Sacred Chorus

EDITED BY JOHN

MUSIC DEPARTMENT

OXFORD
UNIVERSITY PRESS

OXFORD
UNIVERSITY PRESS

Great Clarendon Street, Oxford OX2 6DP, England

Oxford University Press is a department of the University of Oxford.
It furthers the University's aim of excellence in research, scholarship,
and education by publishing worldwide

Oxford is a registered trade mark of Oxford University Press
in the UK and in certain other countries

ISBN 978-0-19-351882-7

Music originated in Sibelius
Printed in Great Britain on acid-free paper by
Halstan & Co. Ltd, Amersham, Bucks

Organ accompaniments for the music contained in this book are in the companion volume,
Sacred Choruses: organ accompaniment book (ISBN 978-0-19-351883-4)

Orchestral scores and parts are available on rental (see the *Index of Orchestrations* on p. 380)

PREFACE

For this, the seventh volume in the *Oxford Choral Classics* series, the aim remains as it has always been: to offer choirs a practical and inexpensive working library of standard repertoire in new, reliable editions, based wherever possible on primary sources. Where space allows, music that is less widely known but of special value within its genre is also included. Inevitably, any anthology is a personal selection reflecting the perspective of its editor, and it must also be recognized that there are wide national differences of repertoire: standard fare in one country may be little known in another. In general, I have selected pieces which are regarded as classics, or which give me particular pleasure. Hence, familiar cornerstones of the repertoire such as Handel's *Zadok the priest* and Brahms's *How lovely is thy dwelling place* are found alongside rarities such as Mendelssohn's *Daughters of Zion* and Lili Boulanger's exquisite *Pie Jesu*, which I hope others will enjoy as much as I do. In the years which have elapsed since the publication of *European Sacred Music* in 1996 it has been gratifying to see some of the rarities in that volume become standard repertoire.

The present *Sacred Choruses* volume can only hope to be representative, not comprehensive. The 384-page extent of the *Oxford Choral Classics* books is close to the practical limit of what singers can comfortably hold in the hand; in the *European Sacred Music* volume it allowed for the inclusion of 54 items but, sacred choruses tending to be longer and more space-consuming than motets, only 28 items would fit into the present volume. Rather than lament what is not in the book, I hope choirs will welcome what *is* in the book. In order to make the choices manageable, the policies I have followed have been these:

1. The period covered is approximately from Monteverdi to Elgar: sacred choral repertoire earlier than the 17th century tends to consist of *a cappella* motets and masses (covered in the *European Sacred Music* volume), while music later than the early 20th century is subject to considerations of copyright and likely to make a book such as this more expensive. The geographic area covered is reluctantly limited to Britain and some of mainland Europe. It is hoped that a later volume will rectify some of the omissions.

2. Only music originally written for mixed voices with orchestral accompaniment is included, except for the Lili Boulanger *Pie Jesu* which is for solo soprano with small ensemble (adapted here to include a choir part), and the Satie *Kyrie eleison* which is accompanied by organ. Orchestral scores and parts to match the vocal scores in this book are available from the Oxford University Press hire library or appropriate agent.

3. Extracts from longer works such as masses, requiems, and oratorios are included if they are effective when detached from their context or have become well known in their own right. The plague choruses from Handel's *Israel in Egypt* are magnificent, but best heard in the context of the whole oratorio. Elgar's *The Spirit of the Lord* is a firm favourite as a cathedral anthem; other movements from *The Apostles* are not.

4. This book being intended as much for cathedral and church choirs as for concert choirs, I have favoured (with the exception of the *Judas Maccabaeus* excerpts) pieces with texts that are usable in liturgical worship. Settings of Mass movements are not generally used as anthems in Anglican worship, which has regretfully ruled out (for example) some fine Haydn and Mozart inclusions.

5. I have favoured pieces useful in concerts as companions to familiar longer works. The Monteverdi *Gloria* or the Durante *Magnificat* make splendid curtain-raisers to the ever-popular Vivaldi *Gloria*—as does that composer's own *In exitu Israel*. The Purcell *Te Deum* calls for similar resources to Handel's *Chandos Anthems* or *Acis and Galatea* and would fit well in the same programme. The Schubert *Magnificat* pairs well with the Rossini *Petite Messe Solennelle* or a

Haydn or Mozart Mass, and the strangely haunting Satie *Kyrie eleison* makes an interesting alternative to the Fauré *Cantique de Jean Racine* as a prelude to the latter composer's *Requiem*.

6. I have seen no reason to exclude items with solo parts. Concert choirs generally have professional soloists on hand if they are performing major works, and cathedral choirs have able singers in their ranks who welcome solo opportunities such as are found in the Purcell *Te Deum*.

Accompaniments

The piano accompaniments in old editions of choral works can be a sore trial to pianists: too much orchestral detail is often included—and idiomatic orchestral writing may be transcribed too literally, even in such familiar pieces as Handel's *For unto us a child is born* with its all-but-unplayable chains of rapid thirds and sixths. In fact, for the kind of repertoire found in this volume, piano accompaniment is used far more for rehearsal than for performance, and the piano reductions I have prepared are intended primarily for rehearsal use, to be playable and to give support to choirs as they learn the music. On the other hand, performances with organ accompaniment are common, but organists generally have to work out their own organ transcriptions of piano accompaniments which are themselves transcriptions of an orchestral original, a less than satisfactory makeshift. A few highly expert cathedral organists prefer to play, for example, Brahms's *How lovely is thy dwelling place* direct from the orchestral score, but to meet the needs of everyone else, I have prepared a parallel volume of purpose-made three-stave organ accompaniments for the music in this book. In every case these are based on the composers' orchestral originals, and fidelity rather than easy playability is the priority. In my experience, skilled organists relish being given an accompaniment to play that needs practising, provided that it respects the idiom of their instrument.

Editorial considerations

Singing translations have been provided for those pieces where they are likely to be used—an admittedly subjective judgement—and their style of language is intended to match the period of the music, echoing phrases from the 1611 Bible and 1662 Prayer Book where appropriate. Line-by-line translations of all other Latin pieces are shown beneath their piano parts. Titles are given in the language most likely to be used for them in English-speaking countries. Where the singing text is shown in two languages, the same principle has been applied in deciding which text is uppermost. No consistent practice applies: in English cathedrals, *How lovely is thy dwelling place* is generally sung in English, *Insanae et vanae curae* in Latin.

Vocal ranges have not generally been shown; there is probably less need for them when the voicing of the music is for standard SATB choir than there is with multi-voiced *a cappella* motets where decisions have to be made about allocation of voices and possible transposition.

Editorial suggestions of tempo and dynamics have been tentatively added if there are few or none in the original; they are printed small or in square brackets. Crossed slurs and crossed hairpins are editorial, as are small notes (representing continuo realizations) in the piano reductions. Minor inconsistencies of dynamics, articulation, and slurring—all very common in composers' manuscripts and early editions—have generally been corrected without notice, as have obvious errors. Cases of doubt have been footnoted. Where instrumental bass parts are figured, the figuring is shown in the full orchestral scores and continuo parts available with the orchestral material. Original figuring has been editorially supplemented for the lute continuo parts.

Syllabic slurring, the modern publishing practice replacing the earlier custom of separate note stems in vocal parts for separate syllables, has been selectively applied. For seventeenth- and eighteenth-century pieces, slurs have not been added over long melismas, but they have sometimes been added for brief melismas if they help to clarify exact verbal underlay. In later music, phrase slurs for voice parts have been preserved when they are the composers' own.

Orchestral material

Clear, accurate scores and orchestral parts for every item in this book (except for the Satie *Kyrie eleison* which has organ accompaniment) have been newly typeset and are available on hire from the Oxford University Press hire library or its accredited agent. These scores and parts agree in every detail (including rehearsal letters) with the vocal scores in the book. The index of orchestrations (see p. 380) specifies the resources each piece calls for, ranging from just strings and continuo for Durante and Vivaldi to the full orchestras of Elgar and Parry. *Jerusalem* has been included in the book primarily to provide a ready source of the orchestral material for both versions of the accompaniment—Parry's own, and Elgar's more lavish and colourful orchestration, which is available both for full orchestra and in a reduced version which preserves the essence of Elgar's treatment but for much smaller orchestra. Parry's *I was glad*, another favourite on ceremonial occasions, is for the first time available in its full 1911 version, in two scorings: for full orchestra, and for brass ensemble with organ.

Continuo parts

For all pre-1800 items in this book, fully written-out continuo keyboard parts are included in the orchestral hire material, with the exception of Haydn's *The heavens are telling*, which does not really need a continuo. The Schubert *Magnificat*, written for church performance, does however have a figured bass, so an optional continuo part has been provided. Specialist continuo players generally prefer to extemporize their own keyboard parts from a full score or a figured bass; they may wish to disregard the written-out parts provided, but non-specialists will perhaps be grateful for them. A couple of specific policies I have followed should be mentioned: first, the continuo parts have been kept fairly plain and unadorned because experienced players will know how to add their own embellishments; second, it is sometimes wiser to omit ninths, sevenths, and suspensions shown in the figuring where these occur in the music's topmost voice, or at least in a higher octave than the medium tessitura of the continuo part. The effect of suspensions and dissonances doubled by the continuo an octave below where they occur in the choir or orchestra can be unpleasant (a subjective opinion). Some orchestral bass lines are too agile to be readily playable at the keyboard, but I have followed the general custom of showing them exactly as written, leaving it to the player to simplify them as appropriate.

Lute continuo parts (in the form of editorially fully-figured bass parts) are included for the Monteverdi, Purcell, Vivaldi, and Durante items.

Acknowledgements

I am deeply grateful for the advice, help, and encouragement given to me by my musical colleagues whose names are recorded below; they are all phenomenally busy people who have patiently and courteously put their expertise at my disposal. Dr Lynda Sayce, lutenist and musicologist, has tracked down for me many (in some cases obscure) manuscripts and printed sources in the libraries of the world. Andrew Lucas, Master of the Music at St Albans Cathedral, has given valuable advice on the style and format of the organ accompaniments book and been a sounding board for my thoughts. Richard Pearce, accompanist to the Royal Choral Society and freelance organist, has meticulously scrutinized all the piano and organ accompaniments and made innumerable pertinent suggestions. Daniel Hyde, Director of Music-elect of King's College Cambridge, has gone through the entire contents of both books once more and helped me to rectify many shortcomings still remaining. Dr Ruth Smith has kindly clarified a number of historical points arising in the Handel items, as has Professor John Butt for the Bach items. Brian Jones, organist emeritus of Trinity Church Boston, has given me the benefit of a wise and experienced transatlantic perspective on the project. Of my many friends at Oxford University Press I especially want to thank Ben Selby, head of the music department, and Phil Croydon, senior music editor, for their support at every stage, and finally, my eagle-eyed editor for the project Laura Jones, who misses nothing and has been a model of tact in dealing with me.

JOHN RUTTER

1. Gratias agimus tibi

(Grant that our hearts may be thankful)

Words from the Ordinary of the Mass
English version by John Rutter

J. S. BACH (1685–1750)
from the Mass in B minor, BWV 232

Note: all dynamic markings are editorial.

*This note is an A in the original, but is a B—which seems preferable—at the parallel place in the final *Dona nobis pacem*, and in Cantata 29.

2. Jesu, joy of man's desiring*

(*Jesus bleibet meine Freude*)

Words by Martin Jahn (*c.*1620–*c.*1682)
English text by Robert Bridges (1844–1930)

J. S. BACH (1685–1750)
from Cantata no. 147

*Inclusive alternative: *Jesu, joy of our desiring.*

with ____ the ____ fire_____ of ____ life_____ im -
mei - - *ner* ____ *See* - - *le* ____ *Schatz*_____ *und*

- pas - sioned
Won - *ne,*

*The soprano trills here and in bar 59 are generally omitted in performance.

dy - - ing round___ thy___ throne.
Her - - zen und___ Ge - sicht.

(con Ped.)

3. Praise our God who reigns in glory

(Lobet Gott in seinen Reichen)

Words of unknown authorship
English version by John Rutter

J. S. BACH (1685–1750)
from the Ascension Oratorio, BWV 11

Note: all dynamic markings are editorial.

*Exceptionally, in this chorus syllabic slurs are shown as for the English version only, in the interests of avoiding the use of many dotted slurs.

**This appoggiatura (taking the value of a ♪) is in the 1st violin part only, but could be added to the soprano part here and in bar 147.

Bar 93, vocal bass: last note amended from D in source.

Bar 125, vocal bass: last note amended from G in source.

4. Subdue us by thy goodness

(Ertöt uns durch dein Güte)

Words by Elisabeth Creutziger (1524)
English version by John Rutter

J. S. BACH (1685–1750)
from Cantata no. 22

*Dynamics are left to the discretion of the conductor (there are none in the original). If preferred, the accompanist can play just the top and bottom parts, omitting the middle parts, which derive from the second violin and viola.

-fess - ing   In
-geh - ren   *Und*

thank - ful   hymns_   of___   praise.
G'dan - ken   *hab'n_*   *zu___*   *dir.*

5. Creation's Hymn
(*Die Ehre Gottes aus der Natur*)

Words by C. F. Gellert (1715–69), based on Psalm 19
English version by John Rutter

L. van BEETHOVEN (1770–1827), Op. 48 no. 4
Choral adaptation by John Rutter

*The piano accompaniment is Beethoven's own.

6. Pie Jesu

Words from the Missa pro defunctis

LILI BOULANGER (1893–1918)
arranged by John Rutter

*This piece was scored for solo soprano, string quartet, harp, and organ. The purpose of the optional choir part in this arrangement is to substitute for string quartet in performances with organ alone. Choirs in Dec./Can. formation could assign the solo soprano part to all the sopranos on one side, with sopranos on the other side singing the choral soprano part.

**If preferred, the soprano part could be omitted in bars 1–9.

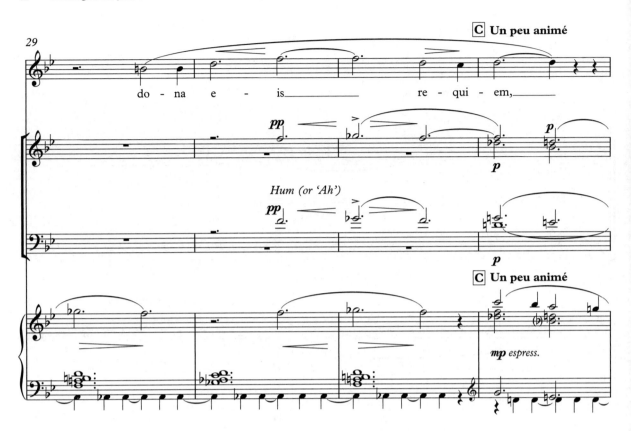

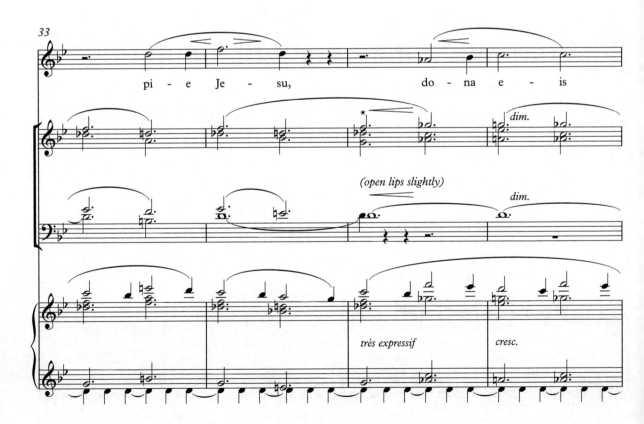

*If preferred, 2nd sopranos can take the upper alto part until bar 38, altos all singing the lower alto part.

eternal rest.

sem - pi - ter - nam   re -   -   qui - em.   A -

- - - - men.

7. How lovely is thy dwelling place

(Wie lieblich sind deine Wohnungen)

Words from Psalm 84
Translation: cento

JOHANNES BRAHMS (1833–97)
from *Ein deutsches Requiem*, Op. 45

*D in source, probaly a misprint.

8. Magnificat
for five voices

Canticle of the BVM
(Luke 1: 46–55)

FRANCESCO DURANTE (1684–1755)
(formerly attributed to Pergolesi)

**My soul doth magnify the Lord:

*The piano part is intended only for use in rehearsal. The music is scored for first and second violins, cello, and bass, with continuo organ, but Durante's highly idiomatic, often antiphonal interplay of the two violin parts cannot be adequately represented at the keyboard. The two violin parts in bars 1–78, 93–152, and 198–255 are shown in outline in the small stave above the piano part, for information; adept pianists may be able to play some of them while still encompassing the continuo bass. Performance accompanied by organ alone is not recommendable either, but in situations where no orchestra is available, it is highly effective to perform the piece with two (or three) solo violins—an additional solo violin plays in the section from bars 153–172 but its part can be taken by the first violin—and chamber organ, plus cello if available. The full score, string parts, and continuo organ part are available for purchase: full score (978-0-19-352747-8); set of parts (978-0-19-352748-5).

**Translation from the 1662 Book of Common Prayer.

and my spirit hath rejoiced in God my Saviour.

For he hath regarded the lowliness of his hand-maiden.

For behold, from henceforth all generations shall call me blessed.

For he that is mighty . . .

*This marking is in the autograph.

And his mercy is on them that fear him throughout all generations.

He hath shewed strength with his arm:

he hath scattered the proud

in the imagination of their hearts.

He hath put down the mighty from their seat: *and hath exalted the humble and meek.*

He hath filled the hungry with good things: and the rich he hath sent empty away.

He remembering his mercy hath holpen [helped]his servant Israel:

As he promised to our forefathers,

Abraham and his seed, for ever.

*B♭ in ms.

As it was in the beginning,   is now,   and ever shall be:

9. The Spirit of the Lord

Isaiah 61: 1–3

EDWARD ELGAR (1857–1934)
from *The Apostles*, Op. 49

*L (Elgar's marking) = largamente – with some broadening of tempo.

10. In paradisum

Antiphon from the Burial Service
English translation by John Rutter

GABRIEL FAURÉ (1845–1924)
from the *Requiem*, Op. 48

*The original organ part being readily playable at the piano, it is shown here exactly as the composer wrote it.

11. Psalm 150

French version of unknown authorship
English version by John Rutter

CÉSAR FRANCK
(1822–90)

12. For unto us a child is born

Isaiah 9: 6

G. F. HANDEL (1685–1759)
from *Messiah*

Note: dynamic markings are editorial.

*Handel's own marking.

*F♯ in source.

13. Hallelujah

Revelation 19, 6; 11, 15; 19, 16

G. F. HANDEL (1685–1759)
from *Messiah*

Note: all dynamic markings are editorial.

14. Let their celestial concerts all unite

Words by Newburgh Hamilton (1691–1761)

G. F. HANDEL (1685–1759)
from *Samson*

In *Samson*, this chorus follows directly on from the soprano aria *Let the bright seraphim*.

Note: all dynamic markings are editorial.

15a. See, the conqu'ring hero comes

*Words of unknown authorship

G. F. HANDEL (1685–1759)
from *Judas Maccabaeus*

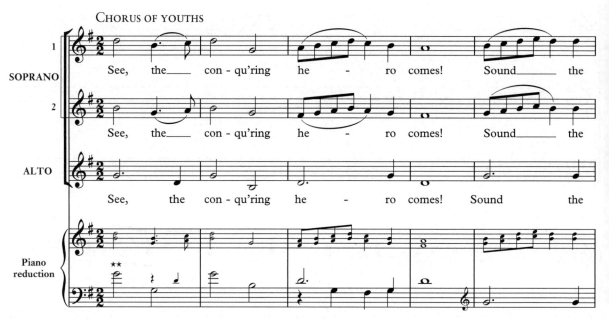

**From here to bar 32 the small notes (doubling voice parts) have been editorially added.

*This chorus was originally written for *Joshua* (1747), for which oratorio the librettist is unknown.

Lyrics:

See the god-like youth advance! Breathe the flutes, and lead the dance. Myr-tle wreaths, and ro-ses twine, To deck the he-ro's brow divine, Myr-tle wreaths, and

*lead the dance.

*Editorial alternative.

*Editorial alternative.

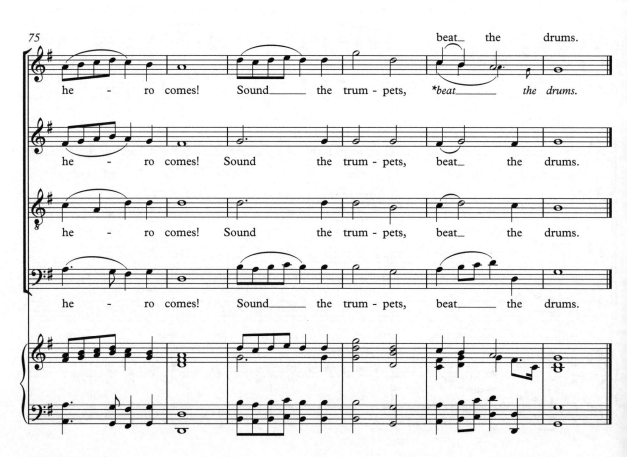

*Editorial alternative.

15b. March⋆

G. F. HANDEL (1685–1759)
from *Judas Maccabaeus*

Piano
reduction

⋆This follows *See, the conqu'ring hero* in Handel's running order (leading into *Sing unto God*) but it may be preferable for it to be played first, as an introduction. It could be played again, without repeats, after *See, the conqu'ring hero.*

15c. Sing unto God

Words by
Thomas Morell (1703–84)

G. F. HANDEL (1685–1759)
from *Judas Maccabaeus*

Sing un - to God, and high af - fec - tions raise, to crown this con-quest with un-mea - sur'd praise,

Note: all dynamic markings are editorial.

16. Zadok the priest

(Coronation Anthem No. 1)

1 Kings 1, 38–40

G. F. HANDEL
(1685–1759)

Note: dynamic markings throughout are editorial, except for Handel's markings 'soft' in bar 1 and 'loud' in bar 23.

17. Insanae et vanae curae

(My spirit is sore afflicted)

Words of unknown authorship
English version by John Rutter

F. J. HAYDN
(1732–1809)

*The rhythm is clearly given in the source as ♩♩ but some editions amend it to ♩.♩ here and in parallel places.

*Editorial appoggiatura.

18. The heavens are telling the glory of God

(*Die Himmel erzählen die Ehre Gottes*)

Text paraphrased from Psalm 19: 1–4

F. J. HAYDN (1732–1809)
from *The Creation*

tell - ing the glo - ry of God;   the won - der of his works,   the
-zäh - len die Eh - re___ Got - tes; und sei - ner Hän - de Werk,   und

tell - ing the glo - ry of God;   the won - der of his___
-zäh - len die Eh - re Got - tes;   und sei - ner Hän - de___

glo - ry of God;   the won - der,   the won - der of his___
Eh - re___ Got - tes; und sei - ner,   und sei - ner Hän - de___

glo - ry of God;   the won - der, the won - der of his works,   the
Eh - re___ Got - tes; und sei - ner, und sei - ner Hän - de Werk,   und

won - der of his works   dis - plays the fir - ma - ment,   the
sei - ner Hän - de Werk   zeigt an das Fir - ma - ment,   und

works   dis - plays,   dis - plays the fir - ma - ment,   the won - der of his___
Werk   zeigt an,   zeigt an das Fir - ma - ment,   und sei - ner Hän - de___

works   dis - plays,   dis - plays the fir - ma - ment,   the won - der of his___
Werk   zeigt an,   zeigt an das Fir - ma - ment,   und sei - ner Hän - de___

won - der of his works   dis - plays the fir - ma - ment,   the
sei - ner Hän - de Werk   zeigt an das Fir - ma - ment,   und

* ♩ in source.

123

The won - der of his works dis - plays the fir - ma -
Und sei - ner Hän - de Werk zeigt an das Fir - ma -

of his works dis - plays the fir - ma - ment.
Hän - de Werk zeigt an das Fir - ma - ment.

-plays the fir - ma - ment. The won - der of his works dis -
an das Fir - ma - ment. Und sei - ner Hän - de Werk zeigt

-plays the fir - ma - ment. The won - der of his works, the
an das Fir - ma - ment. Und sei - ner Hän - de Werk, und

127

-ment, the fir - ma - ment.
-ment, das Fir - ma - ment.

The won - der of his works_____ dis-plays the fir - ma -
Und sei - ner Hän - de Werk_____ zeigt an das Fir - ma -

-plays the fir - ma - ment. The won - der of his works dis - plays the_ fir - ma -
an das Fir - ma - ment. Und sei - ner Hän - de Werk zeigt an das_ Fir - ma -

won - der of his works dis - plays the fir - ma - ment, dis -
sei - ner Hän - de Werk zeigt an das Fir - ma - ment, zeigt

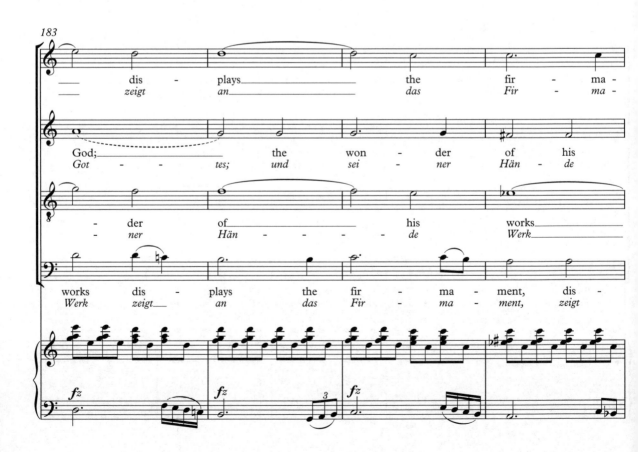

19. Daughters of Zion

Luke 23: 28–30

(*Ihr Töchter Zions*)

FELIX MENDELSSOHN (1809–47)
from *Christus*, Op. 97

20. Gloria

for seven voices

Words from the Ordinary of the Mass

CLAUDIO MONTEVERDI
(1567–1643)

Note: all dynamic markings and slurs are editorial.

*See commentary for discussion of the solo–tutti markings.

*The Cs in S.1 and Vln 1 have a ♯ added by hand in the source, which avoids the false relation with the bass, but is not necessarily preferable.

**These four bars are in the alto part-book (probably a printer's error), but it is suggested they be reassigned to basses 1 and 2 as shown.

And on earth peace . . .   *to men of good will.*

*The ♯ was added by hand in the source. ♮ may be considered preferable.

We give thanks . . . to you

because of your great glory.

*The small notes here and in bars 154, 166, and 192 are editorial ornaments.

heavenly King, God the Father Almighty.

O Lord, the only-begotten Son . . .

Jesus Christ,

Lamb of God, Son of the Father,

Ritornello [Poco meno mosso]

have mercy upon us.

TENOR 1 [Solo] *mp*

TENOR 2 [Solo] *mp*

You who take away . . .

the sins of the world,

receive,

*This G is probably correct, though it could be a misprint for A one note higher.

21. Lacrimosa

Words from the *Missa pro defunctis*

W. A. MOZART (1756–91)
from *Requiem*, K626

juー diー canー dus　 hoー mo　 reー us,　 laー criー moー sa

juー diー canー dus　 hoー mo　 reー us,　 laー criー moー sa

juー diー canー dus　 hoー mo　 reー us,　 laー criー moー sa

juー diー canー dus　 hoー mo　 reー us,　 laー criー moー sa

man to be judged as defendant.

diー es ilー la,　 quaー reー surー get　 exー faー vilー la

diー es ilー la,　 quaー reー surー get　 exー faー vilー la

diー es ilー la,　 quaー reー surー get　 exー faー vilー la

diー es ilー la,　 quaー reー surー get　 exー faー vilー la

★ ♩. in source.

grant them rest.

22. Laudate Dominum

(Lord God, we praise thy Name)

Psalm 117
English version by John Rutter

W. A. MOZART (1756–91)
from the *Solemn Vespers*, K339

23. Jerusalem

Words by
William Blake (1757–1827)

C. HUBERT H. PARRY
(1848–1918)

*The piano accompaniment is Parry's own. In bar 6 there is no C♯ on beat 2 in the orchestral version.
**In Elgar's version, verse 1 is directed to be sung by sopranos and altos, verse 2 by all voices.
Note: three versions of the full score and parts are available on hire (see index of orchestrations, p. 380).

★***p*** in both Parry's and Elgar's orchestral versions.

*The two lower notes are taken from Parry's orchestral version.

24. I was glad when they said unto me

(1911 version)

Psalm 122: 1–3, 6, 7

C. HUBERT H. PARRY
(1848–1918)

*This extra beat is not in the 1911 full score, but it is in all versions of the vocal score.

*The dotted rhythm in Soprano 1 here is clear in the autograph full score but is changed to equal quavers in the 1902 vocal score, and in all subsequent vocal scores. Parry may have made the change at proof stage, but proofs are no longer extant, so it remains uncertain.

*(optional cut to G on p. 296)

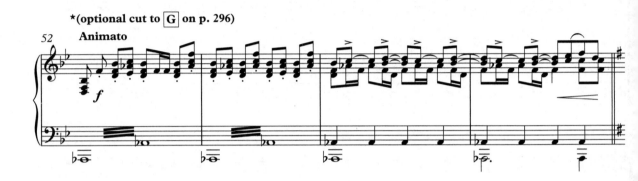

†KING'S SCHOLARS OF
WESTMINSTER SCHOOL

Vi - vat Re-gi - na Ma- ri - a!   Vi - vat Re-gi - na Ma- ri - a!   Vi - vat! Vi - vat!
**Glo - ry to God in the high-est!   Glo - ry to God in the high-est!   Glo-ry! Glo-ry!

*Composer's note: 'When the traditional Vivats are impractical a cut can be made from * to letter G'.

**Alternative, editorial text for general use.

†See commentary for performance suggestions.

*The 1902 and 1911 vocal scores have 'semi-chorus or quartet'. The 1911 full score has no special indication.

*The lower notes may have been intended as alternatives, but both notes are generally sung.

25. Te Deum

(D major setting)

Words from the 1662 Book of Common Prayer

HENRY PURCELL
(1659–95)

Note: dynamic markings are editorial.

58

*Purcell's own instruction.

*Editorial appoggiatura.

*Editorial appoggiatura.

*Editorial appoggiatura.

*Editorial appoggiatura.

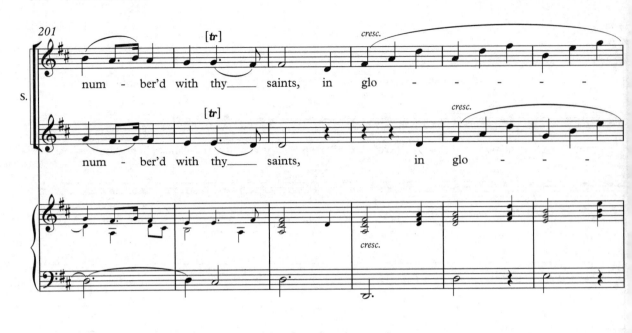

num - ber'd with thy____ saints, in glo - - - - -

num - ber'd with thy____ saints, in glo - - -

- - ry ev - er - last - ing.

- - ry ev - er - last - ing.

ALTO 1 SOLO
O   Lord,   save,

ALTO 2 SOLO
O   Lord,   save,

BASS SOLO
O   Lord,   save,

*Editorial appoggiatura.

*In non-liturgical performances the piece could end here if it needs to be abridged.

26. Kyrie eleison

Words from the Ordinary of the Mass

ERIK SATIE (1866–1925)
from *Messe des pauvres*

*There are no barlines in the original. The editorial short barlines are purely to guide the eye and have no metrical or phrasing significance.

*E in source, but C♯ more likely.

GRAND ORGUE

ORGUE DU CHŒUR

LOWER VOICES

Ky - ri - e   e - le - i - son

27. Magnificat

Canticle of the BVM
(Luke 1: 46–55)

FRANZ SCHUBERT (1797–1828)
D486

*My soul doth magnify the Lord:

and my spirit hath rejoiced in God my Saviour.

Translation from the 1662 Book of Common Prayer

For he hath regarded the lowliness of his hand-maiden.

For behold, from henceforth all generations shall call me blessed.

He hath put down the mighty . . .

from their seat: and hath exalted the humble and meek.

He hath filled the hungry with good things: and the rich he hath sent empty away.

As he promised to our forefathers,

Abraham and his seed, for ever.

E **Allegro vivace**

Choir Glo - ri - a Pa - tri, et Fi - li - o, et Spi - ri - tu - i

Glory be to the Father, and to the Son, and to the Holy Ghost:

San - cto. Si - cut e - rat in prin - ci - pi - o, et nunc, et

As it was in the beginning, is now, and ever shall be:

28. In exitu Israel

(When Israel departed from Egypt's land)

*Psalms 114 and 115
English translation by John Rutter

ANTONIO VIVALDI
(1678–1741)

*Psalm 113 according to Catholic numbering.

ve - stros.　Be - ne - di - cti　vos a　Do － mi - no, qui fe - cit　cae - lum et
chil - dren;　*For the Lord who*　*made the*　*heav'n*　*and earth hath*　*grant - ed*　*thee his___*

ter - ram, et ter － ram.　Cae - lum　cae - li　Do - mi - no:　ter - ram
bless - ing for ev - er - more.　*All the*　*hea - vens are the Lord's,*　*but the*

au - tem de - dit fi - li - os ho - mi - num.　Non mor - tu - i　lau -
earth hath he cre - a - ted for mor - tal man.　*The dead rise not to*

-da - bunt te Do - mi - ne: ne-que om-nes qui de-scen-dunt in in - fer - num. Sed nos qui
praise thee, O Lord of hosts, nei-ther all who have de-scend-ed in - to si - lence. But we the

vi - vi-mus, be - ne - di - ci-mus Do-mi - no, ex hoc nunc et us-que in sae - cu - lum.
liv - ing shall bless the Name of the Lord of hosts from this time forth for ev - er and ev - er - more.

Glo - ri - a Pa - tri, et Fi - li - o, et Spi - ri - tu - i San - cto. Si - cut
Glo - ry be to the Fa - ther, Son, and Ho - ly Spi - rit, As it

COMMENTARY

1. Bach: *Gratias agimus tibi*

This is the seventh movement of Bach's *Missa* of 1733, which was later incorporated into his *Mass in B minor* (a title not bestowed until the nineteenth century). With only minimal adaptation, the music recurs as the concluding *Dona nobis pacem* in the complete Mass—which dates from the late 1740s, towards the very end of Bach's life. The *Gratias* is itself a recycled composition: Bach first wrote the music in 1731 to the words 'Wir danken dir, Gott, wir danken dir' (We thank thee, God, we thank thee) as the opening chorus of the cantata of that name, no. 29, written to celebrate the election of a new Leipzig town council. The Latin re-texting for incorporation into Bach's *Missa* followed two years later. Its style is archaic—the *stile antico*, strictly contrapuntal and motet-like—with instrumental parts that essentially just double the voice parts except when the trumpets take off into a crowning final fugue entry of their own. Given that the text to which Bach originally set the music expressed the idea of thanksgiving rather than peace, the 'Gratias' rather than the 'Dona nobis pacem' version is chosen here. *Source: autograph manuscript, Berlin, Staatsbibliothek, Mus.ms. Bach P 180.*

2. Bach: *Jesu, joy of man's desiring (Jesus bleibet meine Freude)*

Several hands contributed to the creation and propagation of this, perhaps the best-loved of Bach's elaborated chorales which are a feature of a number of his church cantatas. The hymn tune on which it is built, *Werde munter, mein Gemüte*, was composed—in duple time—by the 17th-century Hamburg-based violinist/composer Johann Schop, and became well known in the Lutheran world following its appearance in a 1642 hymn collection co-edited by him. Bach used it in the *St Matthew Passion* and in four cantatas, of which the present one, no. 147, *Herz und Mund und Tat und Leben*, is the best known. To fit in with the cantata's liturgical use at the Feast of the Visitation, he discarded the original text, choosing instead two stanzas from a nineteen-verse hymn of 1661 by the German poet and musician Martin Jahn. The whole movement was an afterthought: the cantata was composed in 1716 at Weimar without it. It was added in 1723 in Leipzig, together with three new recitatives, when Bach made a revised version in which it appears twice, once at the close of Part I to the words of the sixth stanza, and again, musically identical, at the close of Part II, to the words of stanza 17, *Jesus bleibet meine Freude*. The English words were written by the Poet Laureate Robert Bridges in the early twentieth century. His text is closer in meaning to stanza 17 than to stanza 6, but it is not a translation as such, more of an invention inspired by Jahn's hymn as a whole.

Wider fame for *Jesu, joy of man's desiring* in the English-speaking world was to follow when the pianist Myra Hess published a piano transcription in 1926 which she recorded in 1940, a best-seller in both forms. The reverent, spiritual style of her performances of the piece (often featured at her morale-boosting National Gallery concerts during World War II) was influential and took Bach's composition far from his likely intention, which was that the music would be joyful and almost jig-like—the chorale melody is doubled by trumpet, suggesting extrovert, festive performance—but the universality of his genius allows for many interpretations. *Source: autograph manuscript, Berlin, Staatsbibliothek, Mus.ms. Bach P 102.*

3. Bach: *Praise our God who reigns in glory (Lobet Gott in seinen Reichen)*

One of the finest of a whole family of joyful, celebratory Bach choruses with rich orchestral accompaniments including trumpets, *Lobet Gott in seinen Reichen* opens the 1735 Ascension Oratorio (Bach's title was *Himmelfahrts-oratorium*), a work which followed hard on the heels of the Christmas Oratorio of 1734 but is shorter and not really an oratorio as the term is now understood but rather a two-part cantata—the old BG edition styled it as Cantata no. 11. The text, probably by Bach's regular literary collaborator C. F. Henrici (pen name Picander), draws on imagery from Psalms 148–150 in the opening chorus, but as was convincingly demonstrated by the Bach scholar André Pirro in his 1907 book *The aesthetics of Johann Sebastian Bach*, it fits the music less closely than an earlier, secular text for which Pirro believed the music to have been composed. This was an ode, *Froher Tag, verlangte Stunden*, written to celebrate the building of an extension to St Thomas's School in 1732. The text, by a local Leipzig poet, is extant; Bach's music is lost, but if it was indeed the source of the *Lobet Gott* chorus we can only marvel that a mundane occasion called forth music of such splendour. *Source: autograph manuscript, Berlin, Staatsbibliothek, Mus.ms. Bach P 44.*

4. Bach: *Subdue us by thy goodness (Ertöt uns durch dein Güte)*

Almost as beloved as *Jesu, joy of man's desiring*, this closing movement from Cantata no. 22, *Jesus nahm zu sich die Zwölfe*, is a slightly earlier example of the same technique: take a chorale well-known to a Lutheran congregation and add to it an instrumental accompaniment of some elaboration, the chorale appearing line by line, with breaks in between, while the accompaniment continues seamlessly on. In this case the accompaniment is itself a melody of heart-melting beauty, and the chorale a fine one dating from the fifteenth century, *Herr Christ, der einge Gottessohn*. The cantata was one of two test pieces submitted by Bach in 1723 in support of his application for the post of Cantor at St Thomas's Church, Leipzig (the other was Cantata no. 23, *Du wahrer Gott und Davids Sohn*). He got the job. *Source: autograph manuscript, Berlin, Staatsbibliothek, Mus.ms. Bach P 119.*

5. Beethoven: *Creation's Hymn (Die Ehre Gottes aus der Natur)*

This is no. 4 of a set of six songs with piano, Op. 48, to texts by the German pastor and poet C. F. Gellert, published in

1803. Beethoven dedicated the set to the Count von Browne, one of his early patrons. The texts are taken from Gellert's *Geistliche Oden und Lieder* of 1757. The lofty, hymn-like tone of *Die Ehre Gottes aus der Natur*, seeing God revealed in the wonders of nature, was inspired by Psalm 19 (The heavens declare the glory of God), as was Haydn's chorus 'The heavens are telling' from *The Creation*, composed some five or six years before Beethoven's song; both composers held pantheistic beliefs. Beethoven's song gained its most widespread renown in choral adaptations made after the composer's lifetime, and its piano part was orchestrated by the Austrian conductor Felix Mottl (1856–1911), who also made orchestral versions of songs by Mozart, Schubert, Loewe, and Strauss. Turning Beethoven's song into a choral hymn with orchestra was not inappropriate, making explicit the grandeur of a composition which bore the unusual tempo instruction 'majestic and elevated'. *Source: (for the original version with piano) first edition, Vienna, Mollo, 1803; (for the orchestration) published edition (late 19th c.), Leipzig, Breitkopf & Härtel. Gellert's poem has six verses, Beethoven's setting and Mottl's orchestration encompassing only the first two of them.*

6. Lili Boulanger: *Pie Jesu*

Lili Boulanger and her older sister Nadia were born in Paris to an artistic and devoutly Catholic Franco-Russian family. From an early age both sisters showed exceptional musical talent which was encouraged by their parents; Nadia enrolled as a composition student at the Paris Conservatoire, but Lili's short life of 24 years was dogged by ill-health (she suffered from intestinal tuberculosis), and this prevented her from undertaking full-time study, though she accompanied her sister to some classes and studied composition privately. Her composition teachers, Georges Caussade and Paul Vidal, were relatively obscure, but she certainly encountered the music of Fauré, Debussy, and other prominent French composers of the time. The transforming event of her life was in 1913 when, on a second attempt, she won the coveted Prix de Rome in composition, which Nadia had narrowly failed to win in 1908. Lili was the first woman to win this prize (it was for her cantata *Faust et Hélène*) and it made her a celebrity as well as securing her a publishing contract. She spent two fruitful periods at the Villa Medici, composing several vocal, choral, and instrumental pieces, also working on an opera, *La Princesse Maleine*, which remained unfinished. The *Pie Jesu* (1918) was her last composition. Several years earlier she had made sketches for it and for a Kyrie, which suggests she might have intended them to form part of a requiem, but in the event only the *Pie Jesu* was completed, dictated to Nadia because she was too weak to be able to write it down herself.

The forces she wrote it for—organ, harp, string quartet, and solo soprano—belonged to an established nineteenth-century French tradition of church music accompanied by organ plus a small group of instruments (as did the Fauré *Requiem*), but can seem less practical today. With hardly any alteration the string quartet part can be taken by wordless choir, the harp part can be assimilated into the organ part, and if desired the solo soprano part can be taken by *tutti*

sopranos. This fairly minimal work of adaptation opens up a hauntingly lovely and individual composition for performance by choir and organ. *Source: published edition (Paris, Durand, 1922).*

7. Brahms: *How lovely is thy dwelling place (Wie lieblich sind deine Wohnungen)*

This is the fourth movement of Brahms's *Ein deutsches Requiem*, the work which established the international reputation of its 35-year-old composer following its first complete performance in Leipzig in 1869. It is not a liturgical requiem but a setting of passages selected by Brahms from the Lutheran Bible, focusing on the experiences of death, bereavement, and consolation rather than on the souls of departed ones or redemption through Christ's sacrifice; perhaps this was a reflection of the spirit of the age as well as of Brahms's own beliefs. In terms of the structure of the whole work, *Wie lieblich*, a heart-easingly melodious, Ländler-like setting of Psalm 84, serves as a point of relief— its style is not far removed from the composer's *Liebeslieder* waltzes, though with more contrapuntal elaboration. The attractiveness of the music and the absence of any strong textual or musical connection to its context encouraged its widespread adoption as a separate church anthem; English editions were in print before the end of the century and it has remained a favourite ever since. *Source: Brahms, Sämtliche Werke, Vol. XVII, Leipzig, Breitkopf & Härtel, 1926–7.*

8. Durante: *Magnificat for five voices*

Francesco Durante, of whose early life and studies in Italy little is known for certain, settled in Naples in 1728 where he mostly remained until his death in 1755, earning his living by teaching composition at one or other of the four music conservatories in the city, which was then a pre-eminent centre of musical activity in Italy. Unusually for an Italian composer of that time, he avoided opera, concentrating mainly on church music where he gained a high reputation as a master of sacred style, blending the strict contrapuntal *stile antico* with more modern *galant* influences. He was a sought-after teacher; the best-remembered of his pupils was Pergolesi, who began studies with him in 1728.

The dissemination of Durante's music was hampered by the fact that little of it was published, and chronology is hard to establish because his manuscripts, of which many survive, were not dated, and he often recopied or reworked earlier compositions. It is not known when he wrote the present Magnificat for five voices, and it remained unpublished until recent times. However, a much-altered version of it for four voices, almost certainly a later adaptation, was circulated widely in manuscript copies, leading to publication in Germany in the nineteenth century in an edition by Robert Franz. This four-voice version became well-known and was held up as 'in a certain sense the ideal setting of the Marian canticle' by the German music scholar Kretschmar in 1888, its popularity rising further when the Italian musicologist Radiciotti, in a 1911 monograph, declared it, on the evidence of a single secondary manuscript bearing Pergolesi's name, to be a composition by Durante's pupil Pergolesi, whose early death at the age of 26 contributed to a Romantic cult surrounding him. Many works by other composers were misattributed to him; it added to their market value. As a direct result of the Radiciotti monograph, Durante's four-voice Magnificat was included in the complete Pergolesi edition in 1942, since when innumerable performances have taken place of the 'Pergolesi Magnificat'.

The reasons for preferring Durante's five-voice version in the present anthology are primarily that it is vocally richer and more contrapuntally interesting in those sections where the music of both versions runs parallel: the extra voice part makes a difference. The sections where the music was re-composed for the four-voice version are at least as rewarding in the original version, and worth performing as an alternative to the familiar later version—which may or may not be Durante's own work.

The Gregorian chant which forms the *cantus firmus* in the first and last sections is Tone 1 of the various Magnificat chants to be found in the *Liber Usualis* (p. 207). *Source: autograph ms., Naples, Biblioteca del Conservatorio, Rari 1.6.19.*

9. Elgar: *The Spirit of the Lord*

Following criticism of the 'popish' theme of *The Dream of Gerontius* (1900) Elgar determined that the words of his next, long-planned oratorio *The Apostles* should be drawn exclusively from the Bible, avoiding doctrinal controversy. His ambitious plan for a trilogy of oratorios on the theme of the founding of the Christian church, extending to the Last Judgement, was never fully realized, only the first two parts, *The Apostles* (1903) and *The Kingdom* (1906) coming to fruition. 'The Spirit of the Lord' serves as a choral prologue to *The Apostles*, and in a sense to the whole planned trilogy. Its text, from Isaiah, was suggested to Elgar by a reference to it in Longfellow's poem *The Divine Tragedy* which was a major influence on the dramatic scheme of the two completed oratorios. The music of Elgar's prologue must rank as one of his finest achievements of its kind. Paradox, it has often been said, lies at the heart of all great art, and 'The Spirit of the Lord' is filled with it. It feels spacious, as if we are setting out on a long journey together, yet it is concise, lasting under eight minutes. Its mood is hushed and reverent, yet it blazes with passion (bars 30–4) and unshakeable conviction (bars 62–9). The music feels clear and often simple, with choral unisons, yet Elgar manages to set forth many of the complex themes that will run through the whole work (see Jerrold Northrop Moore, *Edward Elgar: A Creative Life*, pp. 384–9). Moore warns us that this should not be too readily equated to Wagner's use of *leitmotiv* technique, which indeed was common to many composers at this time, including Richard Strauss (Elgar and Strauss met and warmly admired each other). Yet Elgar's music in his oratorios would not have been as it was without Wagner, and it is symbolic that Elgar visited Bayreuth the year before *The Apostles* was completed. *Source: autograph ms., London, British Library add. ms. 50819 and first edition, London, Novello, 1903.*

10. Fauré: *In paradisum*

This is the seventh and final movement of the *Requiem*, Op. 48, which remains one of Fauré's best-loved works, first written in 1888 when the composer was organist at the church of the Madeleine; it was intended for liturgical use at funerals held there. It underwent two revisions, the first of them in 1893, expanding it from five movements to seven and slightly augmenting the original scoring—which was for organ with lower strings, timpani, and harp—by adding horns and trumpets. The second revision, published in 1900, was more radical, converting the *Requiem* into a concert work with full orchestra; for many years this was the only form in which the work was known, but circumstantial evidence suggests that Fauré entrusted the revision to a pupil, and in many ways the 1893 version, which remained in manuscript until 1984, is to be preferred, preserving as it does the original liturgical scale and character of the music. (See the preface to the OUP edition, from which this movement is extracted, for more detailed information.) The 'In paradisum' makes an appropriate and moving conclusion to the work, and is perhaps more separable for performance purposes than the other movements because its text is not drawn from the *Missa pro defunctis* but from the Burial Service, the rite traditionally performed after the Requiem Mass itself. *Source: Fauré, Requiem Op. 48 (1893 version), ed. John Rutter, OUP, 1984.*

11. Franck: *Psalm 150*

In 1883 a new 34-stop Cavaillé-Coll organ was installed in the main hall of the École Nationale des Jeunes Aveugles, the French national school for the blind in Paris. Music played an important part in the curriculum—organist-pupils included, at different times, Louis Vierne, André Marchal, and Jean Langlais—and César Franck enjoyed a friendly association with the school, advising on musical appointments and on the specification of the new organ. His Psalm 150 setting was composed for the inauguration ceremony in April 1883, for which an orchestra was available in addition to the organ, plus a choir of pupils from the school. The relative simplicity of the choral parts, although to an extent dictated by the fact they would have had to be learned by rote, was in any case characteristic of Franck's choral writing, which tended to be homophonic and straightforward. The organ, not unexpectedly, is never silent, though its role is supportive more than soloistic. The French paraphrase of the psalm text, apparently written specially for the occasion though its author is unknown, was probably aimed at making the text more accessible to the singers, though being in the vernacular it would have been inadmissible for Catholic liturgical use. Despite this limitation Franck's setting became one of his most widely performed compositions, both within and beyond France. An English version with organ was published in 1898, which encouraged performances in the English-speaking world. *Source: first published edition of full score, Leipzig, Breitkopf & Härtel, 1896. The ms. is lost.*

12. Handel: *For unto us a child is born*

It is paradoxical that *Messiah*, composed in 1741 for Dublin as a work intended for a small choir of professional singers, was so widely adopted by large choirs of amateur singers, remaining in their domain from the time of the giant 1784 Handel commemoration until the period performance movement of the later twentieth century restored it to the smaller scale intended by the composer. Much of the choral writing in *Messiah* can withstand performance on any scale, but 'For unto us a child is born' is not well suited to large forces. It is one of four florid *Messiah* choruses derived from Italian duets earlier composed by Handel (its original text was *Nò, di voi non vo' fidarmi*), and it calls for professional vocal technique. Generations of amateur singers have struggled with its semiquaver runs, and conductors in charge of large-scale performances sometimes allocate these passages to an élite semi-chorus, leaving the full choir to enter with 'Wonderful, Counsellor'. *Source: autograph ms., London, British Library, R.M.20.f.2.*

13. Handel: *Hallelujah*

Probably rather few of the innumerable choristers who have sung this, the most renowned of all sacred choruses, would be able to identify the biblical source of its text (Revelation 19) but in choosing it to close Part II of *Messiah* Charles Jennens, Handel's librettist, surely deserves credit for a dramatic masterstroke. The second part of his three-part structure begins in darkness with the prophetic foretellings of Christ's passion, but, as the theme turns to Pentecost and the propagation of the gospel, something affirmative is needed to celebrate the anticipated triumph of Christian redemption which is the theme of Part III. Handel seized the opportunity and created a four-minute blaze of light: the trumpets, silent since Part I, and the drums, not heard at all up to this point, crown the music with ringing splendour, and as if masterminding a firework display, Handel brings in one new idea after another to ratchet up the excitement. The keyword 'hallelujah' is thoroughly exploited, sometimes set as *Hal*-le-lu-jah, sometimes Hal-*le*-lu-jah, sometimes Hal-le-*lu*-jah. (Endearingly, Handel, who never fully mastered the subtleties of the English language, believed, on the evidence of this chorus and 'For unto us a child is born', that 'for' could be a stressed word.) Realizing he had created a hit, or perhaps just pressed for time, Handel re-used the Hallelujah chorus as the concluding section of his Foundling Hospital Anthem of 1749, *Blessed are they that considereth the poor and needy*. The custom that the audience should stand during the Hallelujah chorus is believed by Burrows (*Handel*, 2nd ed., OUP, 2012) to have originated with the Prince of Wales at this performance, rather than with King George II at a *Messiah* performance: the king, as far as is known, never attended a *Messiah* performance. *Source: autograph ms., London, British Library, R.M.20.f.2.*

14. Handel: *Let their celestial concerts all unite*

A less driven composer than Handel might have allowed himself a rest after the intense labour of composing *Messiah* in 1741, but he seems to have begun work on *Samson*, the largest of his oratorios, almost immediately, sketching most

of it before leaving for Dublin to direct the première of *Messiah*. He resumed work on *Samson* in London in 1742, and the first performance took place, with great success, in February 1743 at the Covent Garden theatre. After the exceptional experiment of *Messiah*, *Samson* reverts to Handel's established pattern of an Old Testament narrative, adapted in this case by Handel's *Alexander's Feast* librettist Newburgh Hamilton from Milton poems, principally *Samson Agonistes*, which in turn was based on the story in the Book of Judges, chapter 16. 'Let their celestial concerts all unite' (its text from *At a Solemn Music*) comes at the end of the oratorio, and it was an afterthought—the 1741 draft had a different finale—as was the soprano aria preceding it, 'Let the bright seraphim'. Perhaps feeling that the new oratorio needed a more upbeat ending than the bible story, Hamilton introduces the character of an 'Israelitish woman', a part taken in the original production by the coloratura soprano Christina Avoglio, who sings 'Let the bright seraphim' which appears to unfold as a *da capo* aria, but which, to great dramatic effect, leads after its B section into the concluding chorus of praise instead of into a reprise of the A section. In concert performance it is worth preserving Handel's scheme, performing the aria, without a *da capo*, before the chorus. *Source: autograph score, London, British Library, ms R.M.20.f.6, and first edition, London, John Walsh, n.d. [1743].*

15. Handel: Triumphal Scene from *Judas Maccabaeus* (See, the conqu'ring hero comes/March/Sing unto God)

As a staunch Protestant, Handel—and much of his public—probably approved of 'Butcher' Cumberland's brutal suppression of the Jacobite rebellion of 1745 which sought to overthrow the Hanoverian monarchy and claim the British throne for the Catholic James Stuart. Sensing a militaristic public mood, Handel created a series of oratorios designed to match it. *Joshua* (1747), to a text by an unidentified librettist, was the third of these, and such was the popularity of 'See, the conqu'ring hero comes', which is heard in the final part, that Handel incorporated it into a 1750 revival of *Judas Maccabaeus*, which had been premièred in 1747 without the renowned chorus—later considered an essential part of the oratorio. A curious little instrumental march reworked from a keyboard piece by Gottlieb Muffat follows 'See, the conqu'ring hero', but is perhaps better placed before it in concert performance in order to provide an introduction. 'Sing unto God', a jubilant chorus in Handel's D major vein to a text by Thomas Morell who was Handel's main librettist in the 1740s, crowns this segment of the drama. *Source: autograph mss. for 'Judas Maccabaeus', London, British Library, ms R.M.20.e.12 and 'Joshua', London, British Library, ms. R.M.20.e.11.*

16. Handel: *Zadok the priest*

This is the grandest of a set of four orchestrally-accompanied anthems composed in a reported four weeks by Handel—possibly on the personal instructions of the king-to-be George II—for George's joint coronation with his consort Caroline in 1727, the only music specially commissioned for the occasion. According to an anecdote recounted by Burney in 1785: 'At the coronation of his late majesty, George the Second, in 1727, HANDEL had the words sent to him by the bishops, for the anthems; at which he murmured, and took offence, as he thought it implied his ignorance of the Holy Scriptures: 'I have read my Bible very well, and shall chuse for myself'. In fact, Handel, having asserted his independence, made the same choice of text for his second anthem—*Zadok the priest*—as Henry Lawes, whose setting, now lost except for the voice parts, was composed for the coronation of Charles II in 1661 and similarly divided into three sections. Although Handel's *Zadok* has always been numbered as 'Coronation Anthem No. 1', it was actually performed second in the order of service, during the Anointing, which has been cited as a possible reason for its extended orchestral prelude, allowing time for the customary changing of the king's robes at that point in the ceremony. In dramatic terms, of course, the richly-scored prelude (marked 'soft' in the ms.) serves to build excitement towards the choral entry (marked 'loud'), and is generally performed as an extended (though twice-interrupted) *crescendo*, which would make it an early and strikingly effective example of a device not generally used until half a century later. *Source: autograph ms., London, British Library, ms R.M.20.h.5.*

17. Haydn: *Insanae et vanae curae*

Haydn originally composed this vivid chorus in 1784 for an expanded revival in Vienna of his 1775 oratorio *Il ritorno di Tobia*. Its text (*Svanisce in un momento dei malfattor la speme . . .*) likens the transient power of a malefactor to the passing of a storm, and it is not known who later wrote the sacred Latin text which converted the piece into a self-standing motet, but it was suggested by H. C. Robbins Landon that in its new sacred guise (presumably approved and overseen by Haydn) it was first performed in 1797 at Eisenstadt, the home of his former prince-patron. The music is similar to Haydn's chorus *Der Sturm* composed for his first London visit in 1792, and to the aria 'Rolling in foaming billows' from *The Creation* (1797): in both cases stormy minor-key openings give way to major-key episodes of lyrical calm. Musical depictions of nature, an established genre at the time, continued into the nineteenth century, Beethoven's *Pastoral* Symphony being a renowned example. *Insanae et vanae curae* was published, with its Latin text, by Breitkopf & Härtel in 1809, followed by various German-text editions. The piece was widely popular in the nineteenth century across Europe, and in England where Novello issued an English-language edition, with a keyboard transcription of the orchestral accompaniment by Joseph Barnby (1838–96). *Source: first edition, Leipzig, Breitkopf & Härtel, 1809.*

18. Haydn: *The heavens are telling the glory of God*

This resplendent chorus with its trio of angels closes Part I of *The Creation* (*Die Schöpfung*), the oratorio Haydn was inspired to write as a result of hearing Handel's *Israel in Egypt* in 1795 while on the second of his two visits to London. On the same visit he received a proposal from the German-born violinist and impresario J. P. Salomon (who had invited Haydn to London) that the composer should

write an oratorio based on the biblical account of creation, to an existing English libretto by a certain now-unidentifiable 'Lidley'. On his return home to Vienna, Haydn had the libretto translated into German, and partially rewritten, by the Viennese court librarian Baron van Swieten. He then composed the music to this German text, and in 1798 the oratorio was performed with triumphant success, first in Vienna under Haydn's direction, and soon throughout Europe.

It was Haydn's intention that his oratorio should be available in both German and English, but the original English text did not always fit van Swieten's German translation, and Haydn, perhaps unwisely, entrusted the far from bilingual baron with the task of adjusting the English text so it would fit the music. The first edition, which Haydn self-published in 1800, had texts in both languages, but the English has often been criticised for its quaintness and sometimes over-literal adoption of German idioms and word-order. The latter can be seen in the present chorus, where the second phrase only makes sense with the inversion reversed, to read 'The firmament displays the wonder of his works', a change sometimes made in performance. Nicholas Temperley (in *Music in Eighteenth-century England*, ed. Hogwood and Luckett) has pointed out that some of the criticism levelled at van Swieten was unfair, in that his English version was often more faithful to its original sources (including the 1611 Bible, Coverdale's Psalter, and Milton's *Paradise Lost*) than 'Lidley' or the German translated from him; and another scholar, Peter Brown (in *Performing Haydn's* The Creation), maintains that there is a strong case for not attempting to 'correct' the English, because, with all its possible faults, it was at least the text which Haydn knew and approved.

Source: original published edition, in full score, of 1800 (a copy of 1803, by which time it appeared under the Leipzig imprint of Breitkopf & Härtel but was otherwise unaltered). The autograph manuscript is lost.

19. Mendelssohn: *Daughters of Zion*

In his second biblical oratorio *Elijah* (1846) Mendelssohn followed Handel's example in taking his subject-matter from the Old Testament, but for what would have been his third he turned to the New Testament, perhaps wanting to affirm the Protestant faith which his Jewish father had embraced on behalf of the whole family. The libretto was compiled from the German Bible by the polymath Christian von Bunsen—biblical and classical scholar, political thinker, and diplomat—who served twice as Prussian Ambassador, first in Rome from 1830–8 where he met Mendelssohn on the latter's grand tour, then later in London from 1839–54 where they met again on one of Mendelssohn's visits to England. It was von Bunsen who suggested to Mendelssohn the idea of an oratorio based on the life of Christ, which the composer began work on during a period in Switzerland in 1847 recovering from grief at the death of his sister Fanny. At the time of his own death in November of that year only a fraction of what was planned as a large-scale work had been completed: a Christmas section comprising a recitative, trio, and chorus (the well-known 'There shall a star from

Jacob come forth'); and two numbers from a Passiontide section (the present chorus 'Daughters of Zion' and a chorale for men's voices). Mendelssohn's brother Paul arranged a performance of the torso, to which he gave the name *Christus*, in Düsseldorf in 1852. Unaccountably, 'Daughters of Zion' never gained the popularity of the Christmas segment, though it shows Mendelssohn at his finest, with the neo-Bachian figure of falling violin pizzicatos aptly evoking teardrops. The English translation (from Novello's publication of the chorus in vocal score later in the century) could well be von Bunsen's own: his English wife and long period in England would have made him bilingually fluent. *Source: autograph ms., Krakow, Biblioteka Jagiellonska, Mus. Ms autogr. Mendelssohn 44/S.*

20. Monteverdi: *Gloria for seven voices*

The Monteverdi scholar Denis Arnold considered the present *Gloria* to be 'perhaps the most splendid of all his church music'. Within its concise time frame and with relatively modest resources, Monteverdi indeed creates thrilling sonorities, strong expressive contrasts, and an overall structure that perfectly reflects the changing moods of its familiar and joyful text. His vocal lines—ear-catchingly tuneful, foot-tappingly rhythmic, and wonderful to sing—are offset by sensuously duetting parts for two violins (which were a novelty in church music at the time).

Monteverdi wrote the work for performance in the Basilica of San Marco, Venice, where he was *maestro di cappella*. The occasion was a Mass, celebrated in 1631 in thanksgiving for the ending of a great plague which had ravaged the city during that year. It is not known how many musicians took part: San Marco had been noted for the sumptuousness of its music, yet now a number of the musicians had died of plague, others were broken in health, and it may be that no more than a handful were left. This could account for the stylistic paradox of the *Gloria*: despite its brilliance and power, it can be performed by as few as ten musicians. It was published in 1641, in the second of his two major collections of sacred music, *the Selva morale et spirituale* [literally, 'Moral and spiritual arbour']. This was a miscellany of liturgical and non-liturgical items composed over a period of time, not as obviously unified as Monteverdi's earlier Vespers publication. As a result, the *Selva morale* has been unjustly overshadowed by its predecessor of 1610.

The *Gloria* can be performed with the minimum resources of seven solo voices, two violins, an optional cello, and a continuo organ. It is equally effective, in a different way, with larger, or even much larger forces. Monteverdi very likely expected the voice parts of at least some of the *Gloria* to be sung chorally. *Solo* and *tutti* markings occur in the part-books, which at first sight seem to indicate the use of soloists as well as choir, though Monteverdi could have been using 'solo' and 'tutti' in the sense of 'this section involves only one voice part' and 'everyone sings here', the markings being intended mainly as cues. Seventeenth-century singers sang not from scores but from part-books containing only their own voice-part, so it was helpful to indicate whether their voice-part was exposed on its own at a given point (*solo*), whether it was one of two or three voice-parts singing (the markings *a 2* and *a 3* are found at appropriate points in the part-books), or whether all the voice parts are singing together (*tutti*). As it happens, it works quite well for the 'solo' sections to be sung by single voices and the 'tutti' sections chorally, but conductors should make their own decision based on the size and expertise of their choir (the 'solo' sections tend to be more florid) and on the acoustics of the performance venue. A possible compromise is to sing everything chorally except for bars 179–235 (and perhaps also bars 141–5, 150–5, and 162–7). This arrangement still calls for six soloists (SSTTBB), but they can be drawn from the choir and can sing from their normal places within the group. Alternatively, the entire work could be sung chorally without any soloists.

The instrumentation of the work is also flexible. In addition to the required two violins and continuo, Monteverdi himself specifies that four trombones or *viole da brazzo* can participate: these would double the lower voice parts in full passages—a convention still observed in Viennese church music more than a century later. There is no reason not to use multiple violins and cellos in larger-scale performances, in which case the selective addition of double bass or violone is desirable. The full score and the cello/bass part of the present edition suggest the places where double bass may most effectively play.

Source: Gloria a 7. voci concertata con due violini & quattro viole da brazzo overo 4. Tromboni quali anco si ponno lasciare se occoresce l'acidente, from *Selva morale et spirituale di Claudio Monteverde (Venice, Magni, 1641)*, 10 printed part-books (*Soprano primo, soprano secondo, alto e basso secondo, tenore primo, tenore secondo, basso primo, violino primo, violino secondo, basso continuo*).

Note: Variants and editorial amendments are listed in full in the separate edition of the vocal score (OCCO 11).

21. Mozart: *Lacrimosa*

According to legend, the opening of this movement from the *Requiem*, K626 (coming at the end of the six-section *Dies irae* sequence) was the last music Mozart wrote from his sickbed before he died in 1791, breaking off at the end of bar 8 and leaving the rest of the movement and much else in the *Requiem* to be completed by his pupil Süssmayr. Mozart's manuscript—consisting of the orchestral introduction and the voice parts—indeed breaks off here, but it is possible that the dying composer discussed his intentions or entrusted sketches to Süssmayr who, once Mozart was safely dead, could well have been tempted to exaggerate the extent of his own contribution to the finished work. Scholars have cited the apparent inferiority of the rest of the 'Lacrimosa', but it exhibits a quality of harmonic subtlety and invention (for example in the dramatic Neapolitan chord in bar 11 and subsequent chromatic shifts) absent in the pedestrian Süssmayr's few known compositions. *Source: part-autograph 'delivery' score, Vienna, Österreichische Nationalbibliothek, m 17561a.*

22. Mozart: *Laudate Dominum*

This is the fifth movement of Mozart's *Vesperae solennes de confessore* (K339) of 1780, a six-movement setting of the texts called for at the Catholic evening service of Vespers. Five of the six movements are psalm settings, the last movement is a Magnificat. Intended for a saint's day celebrating a 'confessor' (one degree down from a martyr in veneration), this quite elaborate and finely-wrought work was the last piece of church music Mozart wrote for the Salzburg court chapel while in the service of the prince-archbishop, prior to his stormy resignation and move to Vienna the following year. There is no evidence that his heart was not in it: in a letter to his father in 1783 he asked for the score to be sent to him in Vienna for him to show to Baron van Swieten, the court librarian, presumably as an example of his skill or in the hope of performance. The 'Laudate Dominum' stands out as an operatic and warmly expressive aria with the chorus almost an afterthought, and it has long been a favourite in its own right. The original soprano soloist (surely female) must have been highly accomplished. *Source: autograph ms., Krakow, Biblioteka Jagiellonska, Mozart Aut. K339.*

23. Parry: *Jerusalem*

By 1916, when Parry composed *Jerusalem*, he was a senior and revered composer in Britain—Elgar had described him in 1905 as 'the head of our art in this country'—which made him a natural choice when the 'Fight for Right' movement, at the height of World War I, wanted a new, uplifting patriotic song. Robert Bridges, the Poet Laureate, had included Blake's little-known poem (the prologue to his epic *Milton*) in an anthology he was editing in 1916 called *The Spirit of Man*, and it was he who approached Parry requesting 'suitable, simple music to Blake's stanzas – music that an audience could take up and join in'. Parry had reservations about what he saw as the jingoistic character of 'Fight for Right' (he actually withdrew his support in 1917), but he complied, and his former pupil Walford Davies conducted the first performance at the Queen's Hall in March 1916. At that stage *Jerusalem* was for unison voices and piano, but its widespread success led to a request for an orchestrated version. This came from the National Union of Women's Suffrage Societies, an organization more congenial to Parry (his wife was an ardent suffragette) and his orchestrated version was premièred in March 1918. With his willing consent it became the official Women Voters Hymn; he died a few months later. Even in the changed post-war climate *Jerusalem* remained popular, and Elgar was asked to rescore it for larger orchestra, for the 1922 Leeds Festival. He retained the unison choral writing (specifying however that verse 1 should be sung by sopranos and altos) but his orchestration is altogether more spectacular and colourful than Parry's own, the 'arrows of desire' sparking off a memorable fusillade of upward-spiralling strings.

Inconclusive debates about the suitability of *Jerusalem* as a Christian hymn and about its possible adoption as a replacement national anthem sprang up in the following years, but today Elgar's *Land of hope and glory* and Parry's *Jerusalem* share the honours as second national anthems. *Land of hope and glory* indeed has a tune that its composer recognized would 'knock 'em flat', but its text, added later by A. C. Benson, is poor stuff compared with Blake, while

Parry's music, carefully crafted in slow three-four time to avoid any hint of a military march, has a metrical elasticity that aptly matches Blake's inspiring text while still remaining 'music that an audience can take up and join in'. *Sources: original version with piano, published edition (London, Curwen, 1916); Parry's orchestral version: autograph ms., London, Royal College of Music, MS 4215; Elgar's orchestral version: two copyists' mss. RCM ms. 7255a and 7255b.* Note: orchestral material for both versions is available from the OUP hire library, also a reduced version of Elgar's orchestration (see index of orchestrations, p. 380).

24. Parry: *I was glad when they said unto me*

This renowned anthem was written for the coronation of Edward VII and Queen Alexandra in 1902, and has been performed at all subsequent British coronations. It is a setting of the Psalm 122 text which opens the service, together with the welcoming cries of 'Vivat' which traditionally greet the sovereign and consort as they process into Westminster Abbey. Despite reported mishaps in the performance, *I was glad* made a strong impression, not least because of Parry's imaginative deployment of the massive forces used in it: a choir of 430 plus the boys of Westminster School who led the 'Vivats', large orchestra, organ, and ten fanfare trumpets. The anthem was requested again for the 1911 coronation of George V and Queen Mary, necessitating a revision of the 'Vivats' to fit the new monarchs' names, and Parry took the opportunity to rewrite the orchestral introduction, replacing the 1902 version with a more richly-scored and thematically relevant one which has superseded the original. For the 1937 and 1953 coronations, the 'Vivats' were necessarily changed, in the 1953 version somewhat to the detriment of the music: bars 60–4 were excised, resulting in a puzzling silence after the final D of the fanfare and an orchestral shift up into A major (for *Vivat Regina Elizabetha*) without a *Vivat* having first been sung in G major. For that reason alone, the 1911 version is much preferable.

The text of the *Vivat* section being appropriate only at coronations, Parry's recommendation for general performance was to omit the whole section. To do this, however, not only makes the anthem too short for its weight and content but also robs the listener of a thrilling moment of musical splendour. To preserve the integrity of Parry's structure, an alternative editorial text for the *Vivat* section has been supplied, based in part on Psalm 150, which enables *I was glad* to be performed complete on any suitable occasion. The part for the King's Scholars of Westminster School is notated in the treble clef, possibly suggesting that Parry had unchanged boys' voices in mind (or a mixture of changed and unchanged voices singing in octaves), but for performances without a special semi-chorus, it may be more effective for this part to be sung by tenors and basses. If a semi-chorus is available, it should if possible be placed at some distance from the main chorus (the Westminster scholars sang from the triforium).

Parry scored the 1911 version of the anthem for large orchestra, organ, and fanfare trumpets which divide into six parts. For the present edition, these six parts are optionally reduced to three, playable by the normal three orchestral trumpets. If organ is available, further instrumental reductions are possible without serious loss to the music (and of course the anthem may be accompanied by organ alone). *Sources: autograph ms. of 1911 full score, London, Royal College of Music, RCM MS 4255, and published vocal scores, London, Novello, 1902 and 1911.*

25. Purcell: *Te Deum in D*

This, the second and more splendid of Purcell's two settings of a text long associated with festive occasions, was composed in 1694 as a pair with his D major *Jubilate* for performance at a St Cecilia's Day celebration in St Bride's Church, Fleet Street, where it was enthusiastically received, soon becoming one of his most popular sacred compositions: many editions were published in the years after his death and it continued to be performed throughout the eighteenth century. Its innovative use of trumpets and its sectional structure with dramatic alternations of solo and choral writing were influenced by the ceremonial music of Louis XIV's court, and in turn influenced Handel's ceremonial music, but, as ever, Purcell speaks with his own distinctive voice, notably in the expressive penultimate section for counter-tenor (a voice Purcell favoured) to the words 'Vouchsafe, O Lord, to keep us this day without sin'. *Sources: copyist's ms., Stanford, California, Stanford University, Memorial Library of Music, ms. 850, collated with first published edition, London, Heptinstall, 1697.*

26. Satie: *Kyrie eleison*

Satie's superficial reputation as an amateurish, reclusive, and eccentric composer who struck gold only with his *Trois gymnopédies* does not stand up to closer scrutiny. He received a sound musical education at the Paris Conservatoire (though he had no good opinion of the institution), was well-connected with the leading artistic lights of *fin-de-siècle* France, was admired by Debussy, and he subjected his compositions to meticulous structural and harmonic planning. It is true that he liked to espouse polemical artistic movements that challenged orthodoxy, and his *Messe des pauvres* (1893–5) dates from a period when he fell under the sway of the Rose-Croix movement of the 1890s, led by the art critic Joséphin Péladan who sought to revive interest in medieval art, religion, myth, and mysticism. Péladin's movement had no direct connection with the Rosicrucian cult, but could certainly be related to the pre-Raphaelite movement in England. The *Messe des pauvres* (of which the 'Gloria' is lost) was one of the main fruits of this involvement, and in the simple diatonic vocal lines of the 'Kyrie' the influence of Gregorian chant is clear. The organ part belongs harmonically to the world of the French musical impressionists, which makes for an oddly affecting conjunction of ancient and modern, not unlike Percy Grainger's folk-song arrangements of a decade or two later. In reaction against the increasing trend for composers to notate every possible detail of performance, Satie, as was sometimes his custom, left no tempo, metrical, or dynamic markings in the *Kyrie*, giving the interpreter great freedom. *Source: published edition (Paris, Salabert, 1920).*

27. Schubert: *Magnificat*

Schubert's considerable output of sacred music has tended to be overshadowed by his other compositional achievements but it was a genre he took seriously and continued with right up to the end of his life. Most of his sacred music, however, dates from his earlier years, including this charming and spirited Magnificat, his only setting of the canticle. It was written in 1815—probably for performance at his own parish church of Lichtental near Vienna, where the organist was his composition teacher Michael Holzer. The occasion must have been a grand one, because the orchestral resources called for, including trumpets and drums, were larger than the normal parish church complement of organ and strings. The music stands in the Viennese orchestral mass tradition of Mozart and the Haydn brothers, whose work the boy Schubert had absorbed as a chorister in the Imperial Court chapel. Characteristics of this style include 'rushing violins' playing *moto perpetuo* scale and arpeggio patterns, supported by block choral parts outlining the harmony, with intermittent passages of contrapuntal interplay. Slow sections are generally song-like. Texts, if verbose, are speedily dispatched or (as with the first section of the present Magnificat) abridged. All these fingerprints are apparent here, contained within a three-movement structure akin to a symphony. The slow movement, with its lyrical oboe solo, would make a delightful short anthem. *Source: first edition, Leipzig, Breitkopf & Härtel, 1888, collated with ms. fragments of two instrumental parts.*

28. Vivaldi: *In exitu Israel*

Viewed purely as a piece of choral music, this high-spirited setting of a vesper psalm seems designed to get through the text in the shortest possible time; it needs to be thought of as a concerto movement with superimposed choir outlining the harmony (a familiar technique in Viennese church music half a century later). The imitative interplay between first and second violins is delightful, the lower string parts have the repeated-note energy associated with Vivaldi's concerto style, and periodic bold unison passages help to articulate the structure. Vivaldi is believed to have composed *In exitu Israel* in 1739 for Easter Sunday Vespers at the Ospedale della Pietà in Venice, the orphanage/school where he had worked, on and off, from 1703 until 1738, first as *maestro di violino*, later being promoted to *maestro de' concerti*. The girl orphans at the Ospedale were widely renowned for the excellence of their musical performances (male participation was not permitted, female tenors and even, implausibly, basses are believed to have been used) and visitors from far and wide came to hear them. Vivaldi wrote a large quantity of music, sacred and secular, for the Ospedale, and although growing fame and his resulting absences led to the termination of his employment in 1738, he was probably commissioned on a freelance basis to write *In exitu Israel* the following year. A set of parts remained in the possession of the Ospedale, suggesting it was performed there, and a payment to Vivaldi for a set of liturgical compositions including six psalms was recorded in April 1739. *Source: autograph ms., Turin, Biblioteca Nazionale, ms Giordano 33.*

INDEX OF ORCHESTRATIONS

Notes:

1. In the orchestral scores, parts for clarinet in C are shown for B flat clarinet, horn parts for horns in F, and trumpet parts for trumpets in B flat or, in certain cases, trumpets in C.
2. ( ) denotes an optional instrument.
3. Continuo parts are listed as optional if the orchestral texture is essentially complete without them.

1. Bach: Gratias agimus tibi
    (2fl), (2ob), (bsn), 3tpt, timp, (cont), str

2. Bach: Jesu, joy of man's desiring
    (Ob), (tpt), (cont), str

3. Bach: Praise our God who reigns in glory
    2fl, 2ob, 3tpt, timp, (cont), str

4. Bach: Subdue us by thy goodness
    (Ob), (cont), str

5. Beethoven: Creation's Hymn
    2fl, 2ob, 2cl, 2bsn, 4hn, 2tpt, 3tbn, timp, str

6. Boulanger: Pie Jesu
    String quartet (optional if choir is used), hp, org

7. Brahms: How lovely is thy dwelling place
    2fl, 2ob, 2cl, 2bsn, 2hn, (org), str

8. Durante: Magnificat for five voices
    Cont, (lute), vlns 1 and 2, (vc), cb (no violas) *Note: the score and parts for this item are available for purchase, not hire.*

9. Elgar: The Spirit of the Lord
    2fl, 2ob, (CA), 2cl, (Bcl), 2bsn, (Cbsn), 4hn, 3tpt, 3tbn, tba, timp, BD, hp, (org), str

10. Fauré: In paradisum
    (2bsn), (2hn), org, hp, solo vln, vla (minimum 3), vc (minimum 2), cb

11. Franck: Psalm 150
    2fl, 2ob, 2cl, 2bsn, 4hn, 2tpt, 3tbn, timp, cym, org, hp, str

12. Handel: For unto us a child is born
    (2ob), cont, str

13. Handel: Hallelujah
    (2ob), 2tpt, timp, (cont), str

14. Handel: Let their celestial concerts all unite
    2ob, 2tpt, timp, (cont), str

15a. Handel: See, the conqu'ring hero comes (Triumphal scene, no. 2)
    2fl, 2ob, 2hn or 2tpt, timp, cont, str

15b. Handel: March (Triumphal scene, no. 1)
    2hn or 2tpt, cont, str

15c. Handel: Sing unto God (Triumphal scene, no. 3)
    3tpt, timp, cont, str

16. Handel: Zadok the priest
    2ob, 2bsn, 3tpt, timp, org, str

17. Haydn: Insanae et vanae curae
    Fl, 2ob, 2bsn, 2hn, 2tpt, 2tbn, timp, (cont), str

18. Haydn: The heavens are telling the glory of God
    2fl, 2ob and/or 2cl, 2bsn, 2hn, 2tbn, (Btbn), timp, str

19. Mendelssohn: Daughters of Zion
    2fl, 2ob, 2cl, 2bsn, 2hn, timp, str

20. Monteverdi: Gloria for seven voices
    (2tbn), (2Btbn), cont, (lute), vlns 1 & 2, (vla), (vc), (cb)

21. Mozart: Lacrimosa
    2 basset hns or 2cl, 2bsn, 2tpt, 3tbn, timp, (org), str

22. Mozart: Laudate Dominum
    (Bsn), org, vlns 1 and 2, vc, cb (no violas)

23. Parry: Jerusalem
    1. *Parry's orchestration:* 2fl, 2ob, 2cl, 2bsn, 4hn, 2tpt, 3tbn, timp, str
    2. *Elgar's orchestration:* Picc, 2fl, 2ob, (CA), 2cl, (Bcl) 2bsn, (Cbsn), 4hn, 3tpt, 3tbn, tba, timp, perc, hp, org, str
    3. *Elgar's orchestration, reduced by John Rutter:* Fl, 2ob, 2cl, bsn, 2hn, 3tpt, timp, hp, org, str

24. Parry: I was glad when they said unto me
    1. *Full orch:* 2fl, 2ob, 2cl, 2bsn, (Cbsn), 4hn, 6tpt (4, 5 6 optional), 3tbn, tba, timp, perc, hp, org, str
    2. *Brass/org:* 4tpt (3rd opt.), 3tbn, tba, timp, perc, or

25. Purcell: Te Deum in D
    (2ob), (bsn), 2tpt, (timp), cont, (lute), str

27. Schubert: Magnificat
    2ob, 2bsn, 2tpt, timp, (org), str

28. Vivaldi: In exitu Israel
    Cont, (lute), str